THE SPICE OF HEALTH

Turmeric is what gives curry its unique flavor and color. It has also been a medical staple in the Indian Ayurvedic medical tradition for thousands of years. Now modern research has confirmed the therapeutic value of curcuminoids, the active substances in turmeric and related plants, and demonstrated their benefits in relief of pain and inflammation, their powerful antioxidant properties, and even their beneficial roles in cancer and AIDS. Learn how this pungent spice can add zest to your health.

ABOUT THE AUTHORS

Muhammed Majeed, Ph.D. holds a doctorate in industrial pharmacy from St. John's University in New York. He has more than 15 years of pharmaceutical research experience in the United States with leading companies such as Pfizer, Carter-Wallace and Paco Research. Dr. Majeed has broad knowledge of the pharmaceutical properties of herbal medicines used in Ayurveda, the traditional system of botanical medicine in India. He pioneered the introduction of several herbal remedies for the European and American markets.

Vladimir Badmaev, M.D., Ph.D. trained in clinical and anatomical pathology at Kings County Hospital and Downstate Medical Center in New York. His Ph.D. is in the field of immunopharmacology. He is the author of many articles and of a book on traditional medicine, with an emphasis on Ayurvedic and Tibetan medicine.

Frank Murray, Editorial Director of *Let's Live* magazine, is the author or coauthor of 30 books on health and nutrition, the most recent being *The Big Family Guide to All the Minerals.*

Turmeric
and the Healing
Curcuminoids

Their amazing antioxidant properties and protective powers

Muhammed Majeed, Ph.D.,
Vladimir Badmaev, M.D., Ph.D.
and Frank Murray

Keats Publishing, Inc. New Canaan, Connecticut

TURMERIC AND THE HEALING CURCUMINOIDS

Copyright © 1996 by Muhammed Majeed, Ph.D., Vladimir Badmaev, M.D., Ph.D. and Frank Murray

This book is a revised and condensed version of *Curcuminoids: Antioxidant Phytonutrients,* copyright © 1995 by NutriScience Publishers, Inc., Piscataway, New Jersey 08854.

ISBN: 0-87983-768-3
Printed in the United States of America

Keats Good Health Guides are published by
Keats Publishing, Inc.
27 Pine Street (Box 876)
New Canaan, Connecticut 06840

C³ Complex™ is a trademark of Sabinsa Corporation

Contents

FOREWORD

Several years ago I was asked to evaluate the safety of a natural yellow dye produced from the spice turmeric. Since I have been researching antioxidants for more than 35 years, I was familiar with turmeric as a natural food antioxidant. I knew that turmeric was indeed safe, but I wanted to show just how safe it was. Unlike many synthetic dyes, natural colorants such as carotenoids and bioflavonoids are safe as well as beautiful. When I investigated the published scientific literature regarding the safety of turmeric, I also took the time to look at the latest research on both turmeric and its unique compounds, the curcuminoids.

My computer search in the National Library of Medicine's Medline yielded more than a hundred scientific articles about turmeric compounds. At the time, Medline contained 193 articles on turmeric and curcuminoids, of which 42 are on safety and toxicity. Also of interest were 16 articles on these compounds as antioxidants, 34 reports on their role against cancer, 23 on their operation in reducing inflammation, five scientific articles on their potential to reduce heart disease and three studies on slowing the progression of the human immunodeficiency virus (HIV) infection to clinical AIDS. In addition to these published studies, there are many private studies such as the Sabinsa studies reported in this book. Fortunately, you won't have to read all of the studies referenced here—as well as later studies since my initial research—as the authors present the information clearly and succinctly so that the reader can understand the totality of the body of science that shows the health benefits of turmeric compounds. Although I did not have the foresight to include turmeric compounds in my laboratory animal studies, I am extremely excited about the research that links modern science to ancient Ayurvedic medicine. Fortunately, these compounds have been in my diet for many years, and I am glad that many of them are now available in supplement form to enhance my antioxidant bioprotection.

The reader may ask, "Why do we need another antioxidant? Aren't vitamins A, C and E enough?" The answer is simple. We can start with a comparison to vitamins. Where would we be if we stopped with Vitamin A and Vitamin B in 1915? Today, we recognize 11 vitamins that are dietary essentials, and several more vitamin-like nutrients. For optimal health, we also need antioxidant nutrients and accessory factors such as carotenoids, bioflavonoids and lipoic acid. Foods contain thousands of beneficial compounds and we should take advantage of those that will help us live better and longer.

There are three good reasons for having several antioxidant nutrients. Antioxidant nutrients work together synergistically. Many antioxidants recycle other antioxidant nutrients that have been oxidized or "spent" in sacrifice to free radicals. Last, and perhaps most important, individual antioxidant nutrients differ in their transport and storage. Some antioxidants act primarily in the aqueous portion of the bloodstream, others within particles of lipoprotein in the blood, others on cell membranes, still others within cellular cytoplasm, and a few in cell nuclei. Antioxidants also vary in their efficiencies to quench various radicals and other reactive oxygen species. The antioxidant profile of vitamin E is different from that of vitamin C, and, likewise, the antioxidant nutrients are partners. Just as we need to eat plenty of fruits and vegetables, we need to get optimal amounts of the major antioxidant nutrients, especially the curcuminoids.

Richard A. Passwater, Ph.D.
Berlin, Maryland

Curcuma longa, also known as turmeric (pronounced tur-muh-rik or too-muh-rik), a member of the Zingiberaceae or ginger family, was highly esteemed by ancient Indo-European people for its golden-yellow color resembling sunlight. This culture, known as *Arya,* worshipped the solar system and attributed special protective properties to those plants, which, like turmeric, produced sun-colored yellow dyes.

Turmeric, best known as *Haridra* in Sanskrit, has a rich history in India, and it has been used for tens of centuries in the Ayurvedic system of medicine. It can be identified by 46 synonyms, such as Pita (yellow), Gauri (brilliant) and other words which signify "night." The reference to "night" may be derived from a tradition which required that married women apply turmeric on their cheeks in the evening, in anticipation of a visit by the goddess Lakshmi. This custom, still practiced in some parts of India, is probably a remnant of an ancient sun-worship tradition. The brilliant yellow color of turmeric found its way into commercial use as a coloring agent for various items, including cotton, silk, paper, wood, foodstuffs and cosmetics.

Turmeric became of special importance to man with the discovery that its powdered rhizome (underground stem or root), when added to various food preparations, preserved their freshness and nutritive value. Turmeric, which belongs to a group of aromatic spices, was originally used as a food additive in curries to improve the storage conditions, palatability and presentation of food.

In Ayurveda, the ancient traditional health and medicine system of India, which dates back over 6,000 years, turmeric has been used internally as a tonic for the stomach and a blood purifier; and externally in the prevention and treatment of skin diseases. Half to one gram was given twice a day for flatulence (gas) and dyspepsia (indigestion). It has been prescribed for liver diseases, particularly for jaundice, as well as urinary tract diseases. In chronic catarrh and coryza (nasal mucus), the inhalation of the fumes of burning turmeric causes copious discharge of mucus and gives instant relief. When boiled with milk and sugar, turmeric has been a traditional remedy for colds.

Turmeric and alum powder in a ratio of 1:20 are traditionally applied to the ear for chronic otorrhea (discharge from the ear). Turmeric has also been described as useful for skin diseases. As an example, the juice of the fresh rhizome is used in parasitic skin infections, and turmeric powder mixed with oil has been applied to soften rough skin. In combination with lime and saltpeter, turmeric has also been applied to bruises, sprains, cuts, infected wounds and inflammations.

In treating pemphigus (a disease characterized by large blisters on the skin and mucous membranes, often resulting in burning and itching), a thick coat of mustard oil and turmeric powder is spread on the skin to alleviate pain and inflammation and to speed up healing. For smallpox and chicken pox, a coating of turmeric is applied to facilitate the process of scabbing. Mixed with borax as a paste, turmeric can be applied to reduce tissue swelling due to inflammation. A mixture of turmeric can be prepared (one ounce of turmeric to 20 ounces of water) and applied as a cooling eyewash, or used as a lotion, to relieve burning in purulent ophthalmia, known in India as "country sore eye."

Turmeric exemplifies an herb for which clinical applications have evolved over time. Until recently, this perennial herb, widely cultivated in tropical regions of Asia—especially in India—was valued primarily as a commercial item for imparting a lively yellow color, as well as an ingredient in most curry powders. In India, the Bengal variety of turmeric is preferred for dyeing purposes, and the Madras variety is generally selected for flavoring purposes. The long-established image of turmeric as a commercial dyestuff and component of curry was partly responsible for overshadowing its importance as a medicinal herb.

The significance of turmeric in medicine has changed considerably since the discovery of the antioxidant properties of naturally-occurring phenolic compounds. The same ground, dried rhizome of *Curcuma longa* which has been used for centuries as a spice, food preservative and coloring agent, has been found to be a rich source of phenolic compounds collectively termed curcuminoids. Curcuminoids refer to a group of phenolics present in turmeric, which are chemically related to its principal ingredient, curcumin. Three main curcuminoids were isolated from turmeric: curcumin, demethoxycurcumin and bisdemethoxycurcumin. All three impart the hallmark yellow pigmentation to the *Curcuma longa* plant, particularly to its roots.

Although the chemical structure of curcumin was determined by Lampe in 1910, it was only in the mid-1970s and 1980s that the potential uses of curcuminoid compounds in medicine began to be extensively studied. The continuing laboratory and clinical research indicates that turmeric and its phenolics have unique antioxidant and anti-inflammatory properties.[1,3-7] Their potential use in the prevention of cancer and in the treatment of infection with human immunodeficiency virus (HIV) are also subjects of intensive laboratory and clinical research.[2,8,9]

These interesting findings on curcuminoids, as well as concerns over toxicity of synthetic phenolic antioxidants— such as butylated hydroxytoluene (BHT) and butylated hydroxyanisole (BHA)—have further stimulated interest in natural phenolics for medicinal and food applications.

Supplements containing turmeric and curcuminoids are becoming more readily available to consumers, providing easy and inexpensive protection to the body from damage inflicted by free radicals. Turmeric is perhaps the most researched spice for medicinal applications, as the accompanying references amply demonstrate. Even as we go to press additional studies are under way that are validating the broad health promoting aspects of this brilliantly yellow spice.

ANTIOXIDANT PROPERTIES

Turmeric and curcuminoids have been primarily recognized for their antioxidant properties. Explaining the antioxidant properties of curcuminoids has to start with the role of oxygen in our body.

Availability of oxygen to the body is crucial for its metabolism, functioning and well-being. Metabolism, however, does not occur without certain costs. These trade-offs for oxygen utilization are known as oxygen by-products. They become waste that pollutes the body and causes damage to our DNA (genetic material which is a blueprint for the cell's command center), proteins, lipids and other molecules in the cell. Even the defense by the body against foreign invasion, like microbial infection, involves a trade-off. In fact, these defense mechanisms naturally produce oxidants which can kill the invading bacteria, but may also cause injury to the body cells the same way any other oxidant does.

Inflammation in the body, as is encountered in the course of certain diseases (e.g., arthritis), infection or wound healing, is nothing more than the outcome of the defense reaction of the body producing oxidants that cause collateral damage to tissues and organs, which in turn results in inflammation. Moderate inflammation is necessary for the healing process; continuous inflammation, however, leads to chronic conditions like arthritis and associated pain.

Another source of oxidants produced by the body is what are called cytochrome enzymes, which are abundantly present in the lungs and the liver, organs that protect the body against toxins entering from air, water and food. Again, trade-offs are involved in this otherwise necessary and useful function of the body. The activity of these detoxifying enzymes invariably results in the generation of oxidant byproducts.

Unfortunately, the body is not only subject to oxidant damage from "inside" conditions, but also from a variety of "outside" influences. An excess of metals like iron and copper, and their salts, may generate oxidants in the body. People who receive and absorb more than the normal amounts of iron, for example, develop hemochromatosis, a condition that results from the accumulation of iron. Such a condition, coupled with the presence of oxidant by-products, increases the risk of cancer and heart disease. Our daily food is a significant contributor to the category of an "outside" oxidant. Besides the above-mentioned examples of iron and copper, many other components of food, like oxidized fats, enter the body as "Trojan horses," ready to inflict their damage.

Another significant source of "outside" influences that generate oxidants in the body is nitrogen oxide, a compound present in smog and cigarette smoke. Oxidants from cigarette smoke have been implicated by the U.S. Surgeon General as a leading cause of cancer, particularly lung cancer, and increasing the risk of heart disease and stroke.

Examples of the most common forms of oxidants generated by the body during normal functioning are superoxide, hydrogen peroxide, hydroxyl radicals and lipid peroxides. The so-called singlet oxygen molecules are an example of an oxidant generated by the body in the course of a defense reaction. Such oxidants are often referred to as "free radicals," because they are "radical" as opposed to the stable molecules, and "free" to start a chain reaction in the body that will destabilize, or make "radical," molecules from surrounding cells. This process, if not stopped, leads to tissue and organ degeneration that will eventually result in clinically manifested conditions such as chronic inflammation, heart disease, accelerated aging, and disorganized cell growth that may result in cancer.

The need for antioxidants, like curcuminoids, to stop free radical damage is well recognized. This can be accomplished by either minimizing or preventing the oxidants' initial formation, or by neutralizing the existing free radicals in the body. As we will learn in this and subsequent sections, curcuminoids, unlike many antioxidants, are capable of both functions, i.e. prevention of free radical formation and intervention to neutralize existing free radicals. Because of their broad mechanism of action, curcuminoids may be aptly referred to as "bioprotectants." They are natural plant compounds that guard the cells, tissues and organs of the body from numerous "inside" and "outside" influences.

To illustrate how free radicals do their damage, the sequence of changes resulting from an injury—due to burns, thermal shock, radiation, etc.—is as follows:

1. The sensation of pain.
2. Phagocyte (the immune-response white blood cell) activation and the production of damaging free radicals.
3. Arachidonic acid release and subsequent production by the body of inflammatory substances (prostaglandins and leukotrienes) which promote production of free radicals.
4. Depletion of antioxidant defense resources, such as glutathione, from the body.
5. Oxidative stress resulting from the depletion of the antioxidant defense mechanisms.

The aging process exemplifies the cumulative result of free-radical damage to cells, tissues and organs. The human body has built-in mechanisms for counteracting free radicals, but, unfortunately, the antioxidant defense reaction is gradually overwhelmed by the aging process, or disease, or both. The inflammation associated with microbial or viral infections, and the progression of cancer, are just a few of the conditions which contribute to the depletion of the antioxidant defense system of the body. Fortunately, some vitamins, minerals, herbs, and their compounds such as phenolics, flavonoids and carotenoids, have the ability to scavenge or neutralize free radicals.

A number of researchers have provided convincing evidence for the antioxidant properties of curcuminoids. Both turmeric and curcuminoids inhibited potent free radicals such as superoxide and hydroxyl radicals.[1] The antioxidant properties of curcumin in preventing lipid peroxidation, which also generates free radicals, are well recognized.[2,3] Unlike other antioxidants, which have more of a "policing effect" on such errant molecules, the turmeric curcuminoids conduct their activity in a more intriguing way. They go "under cover," so to speak, and ally themselves to the potential "troublemakers." By merging with these potential radical molecules, the curcuminoids are able to absorb many of their negative characteristics thus preventing free-radical formation.

In one study, curcumin was shown to be a potent antioxidant in inhibiting lipid peroxidation in rat liver cells.[1] Spice principles, specifically eugenol from clove, and capsaicin from cayenne pepper, were compared to curcumin for their ability to prevent lipid peroxidation. Curcumin had the highest results for inhibiting lipid peroxidation. The same study also included comparison of curcumin to fat-soluble vitamin E. The results showed curcumin to be eight times more powerful than vitamin E in preventing lipid peroxidation.

The biological effects of curcuminoids in counteracting free radicals have been assessed in animal models with inflammation and swelling. Inflammation is known to be associated with increased levels of lipid peroxides and free radicals, which are generated by the liver as well as by inflamed tissues in the body.

Animals fed curcumin showed decreased levels of lipid peroxides and subsequent reduction in the processes of inflammation.[3,4] These studies show that curcumin prevents the production of tissue-damaging free radicals. In tissue culture studies, rat and mouse liver cells incubated in the presence of various concentrations of curcumin reduced the generation of lipid peroxides.[4] Curcumin also prevented oxidative damage and changes of genetic DNA material in cultured fibroblasts (connective tissue cells).[5]

An important corollary of the antioxidant action of curcuminoids is their potential use as natural food additives to prevent oxidation and rancidity of oils and fats during storage and heating.[6,7] Therefore, the use of turmeric in foods prevents the formation of tissue-damaging free radicals. Analyses of the chemical structure of curcumin, the main curcuminoid, and its biological activity, have established that the para-hydroxyl groups in curcumin molecules are essential for the antioxidant activity of curcuminoids.

Chemically speaking, curcuminoids are categorized into a group of compounds known as phenolics. Of the three recognized phenolics of turmeric, bisdemethoxycurcumin is often regarded as the most potent antioxidant, followed by demethoxycurcumin and then curcumin.[2,8] This data is, however, inconsistent with other experiments which indicate that all three curcuminoids possess similar antioxidant activity.[3]

Research by Sabinsa Corporation, a producer of phytochemicals, has showed that, even though the individual curcuminoids exhibit antioxidant properties, the naturally-occurring curcuminoid complex containing the three curcuminoids has proved to be superior in antioxidant activity—preventing free radical formation.[9] *In vitro* studies (in the test tube) indicate that the addition of the individual curcuminoids to the radical molecules resulted in a significant neutralization of free radicals in a dose-dependent manner, with tetrahydrocurcumin being the most effective, followed by curcumin and bisdemethoxycurcumin.[9] (Tetrahydrocurcumin is a hydrogenated product of curcumin.) The potent antioxidant property of tetrahydrocurcumin, combined with its lack of yellow color, renders it useful in neutral-colored foods and cosmetic applications that currently employ conventional synthetic antioxidants.[10] In still another set of studies, it was demonstrated that different compositions of curcuminoid mixtures may have different free radical quenching abilities as well as modified abilities to prevent free radical formation.

Further analysis of turmeric has shown that, besides the phenolics, turmeric is also a source of a water-soluble peptide with antioxidant properties.[11] This compound has been identified as turmerin, a heat-stable noncyclic peptide which has 40 amino acid residues, and is resistant to the proteolytic action of the enzymes trypsin and pepsin. Turmerin, which is found in turmeric at a concentration of 0.1 percent, has been shown in some experiments to be a more potent antioxidant than curcuminoids or butylated hydroxyanisole (BHA). Turmerin is rich in methionine, the sulfur-containing amino acid, and a known antioxidant, which may in part explain the strong antioxidant properties of this compound.

In summary, the antioxidant mechanisms of curcuminoids may include one or more of the following interactions:

1. Intervening in oxidative attacks to restrict or prevent them from happening.

2. Scavenging or neutralizing free radicals.

3. Breaking the oxidative chain reaction caused by free radicals.

Turmeric and its active constituents, the curcuminoids, and the water-soluble peptide, turmerin, have antioxidant properties that effectively inhibit free radical damage in both *in vitro* (in the test tube) and *in vivo* (in the body) conditions.

WHAT THE SCIENTIFIC EVIDENCE SHOWS: OVERVIEW OF LABORATORY AND CLINICAL STUDIES

The successful use of *Curcuma longa* to treat a variety of conditions has generated, and continues to produce, scientific interest in the curative properties of turmeric root. Most of the work has focused on the use of dried extracts, the volatile oil and the active principles, the curcuminoids. Of primary importance was the discovery of the antioxidant attributes of curcuminoids, which are largely responsible for their wide range of pharmacological activity.

As discussed in the previous section, we need antioxidants because oxygen, which is essential to life, is also a highly reactive gas whose destructive effects can be seen in the corrosion of metals, as well as other substances that can be destroyed by "rusting," the popular term for oxidation.

In vitro, curcuminoids were shown to prevent lipid peroxide formation to a significantly higher degree than pine bark extract, grape seed extract or a synthetic antioxidant such as butylated hydroxytoluene (BHT), which is used to preserve fats and oils in food, cosmetics and pharmaceuticals.[1] The curcuminoids used in the experiment (known as C³ Complex), have been shown to be more effective as an antioxidant than each of the components—curcumin, demethoxycurcumin or bisdemethoxycurcumin—used alone

ANTIOXIDANT ACTIVITY

Curcuminoids have been found in clinical studies to be both safe and effective antioxidants. The properties of curcuminoids in preventing buildup of tissue-injuring free radicals, especially the lipid peroxides responsible for cardiovascular disease, are among the better-known antioxidant properties of these compounds.

Cardiovascular disease is caused by the progressive narrowing of the arterial walls. Deposition of cholesterol plaque inside the arterial walls is primarily due to the buildup of oxidized cholesterol in the blood. In clinical studies, peroxidation of blood cholesterol is evaluated by measuring blood levels of lipid peroxides. Giving 500 milligrams of curcuminoids daily to healthy humans for seven days significantly lowered the levels of blood lipid peroxides, as well as the levels of blood cholesterol.[2] The authors of the study, therefore, indicate a possible use of curcuminoids in the prevention of cardiovascular disease.

What does the foregoing information really tell us about the benefits that curcuminoids can have on the heart? Well, for one thing, the lowering of serum cholesterol to safer levels will help prevent arteriosclerosis. For another thing, curcuminoids have the ability to neutralize some of the free radical activity that is believed to be responsible for much of the cardiovascular disease present in society today.

ANTI-INFLAMMATORY ACTIVITY

Another major biological property of turmeric and curcuminoids is their anti-inflammatory activity, which is comparable in strength to steroidal drugs and nonsteroidal drugs such as indomethacin and phenylbutazone.[3-6] Curcuminoids inhibit enzymes which participate in the synthesis of inflammatory substances in the body that are derived from arachidonic acid.[7]

For example, curcuminoids prevent the synthesis of several inflammatory prostaglandins and leukotrienes.[8-10] The overall anti-inflammatory action of curcuminoids is also related to their well-known antioxidant properties. For instance, curcumin has been shown to inhibit lipid peroxidation, a phenomenon associated with antioxidants as well as their anti-inflammatory activities.[11,12] When the anti-inflammatory properties of curcumin were tested in a double-blind clinical trial in patients with rheumatoid arthritis, curcumin produced significant improvement in all patients, and the therapeutic effects were comparable to those obtained with phenylbutazone, a prescription drug known for its analgesic and anti-inflammatory properties.[6]

ANTICANCER ACTIVITY

The nutritional role of turmeric extract and curcuminoids as anticarcinogens in preventing the development of cancer, and as antimutagens in preventing damage to genetic material, has been the subject of recent research.[13-16] Both the turmeric extract and curcuminoids have been shown to inhibit carcinogenesis and mutagenesis in laboratory animals.

Curcumin was also tested in patients with oral cancer.[17] Some of the patients responded with dramatic improvement within days, while others reacted gradually to the treatment. When curcumin was given to a group of chronic smokers, it significantly reduced the urinary excretion of tobacco mutagens (by approximately 40 percent after 30 days), as well as enhancing enzymatic efficacy in detoxifying cigarette smoke mutagens and carcinogens.[15,16]

OTHER ACTIVITIES

In other *in vitro* studies, curcuminoids have also been shown to exhibit antimicrobial properties. Extracts from turmeric containing curcuminoids were found to inhibit the growth of numerous gram positive and gram negative bacteria, fungi and the intestinal parasite *Entamoeba histolytica*.[18]

In laboratory tests, curcumin also exhibited antibacterial characteristics by inhibiting production of aflatoxins, the toxins produced by the mold *Aspergillus parasiticus*, which may grow and contaminate poorly preserved foods.[19] Aflatoxins are potent biological agents, causing injury to the liver which may result in liver cancer.

Upper gastrointestinal bleeding can be a life-threatening complication in patients with gastric mucosal injury. As a possible deterrent to this complication, researchers in Saudi Arabia reported that the oral administration of an ethanol extract of turmeric produced significant anti-ulcer and cytoprotective (protecting of stomach mucosa) effects in animals.[20]

And finally, one of the properties of curcuminoids currently receiving considerable attention is their anti-HIV (human immunodeficiency virus) effect that was demonstrated during *in vitro* and *in vivo* experiments.[21,22] This is further described in the section on turmeric and AIDS.

ANTI-INFLAMMATORY ACTIVITY OF TURMERIC EXTRACT AND CURCUMINOIDS

Inflammation results from a complex series of actions and/ or reactions triggered by the body's immunological response to tissue damage. Many diseases and physical traumas, including surgery, induce inflammatory reactions. Although these reactions are necessary to start the healing process, they too often create an unbearably painful condition which in some cases can even perpetuate the disease.

Steroidal drugs like cortisone, and nonsteroidal anti-inflammatory drugs (NSAIDs), such as phenylbutazone and indomethacin, are used in clinical practice to subdue inflammation. However, many of these drugs have dangerous side effects. On the other hand, curcuminoids and other constituents of turmeric are known for their natural anti-inflammatory activity. In fact, turmeric is one of the oldest natural, anti-inflammatory drugs used in Ayurvedic medicine. Turmeric extract, the volatile oil from turmeric and curcuminoids were said to posses anti-inflammatory activity in different experimental models of inflammation in animal models.[1-3]

The anti-inflammatory and wound healing activity of curcumin was evaluated in a group of patients who underwent surgery.[4] In this double-blind controlled study, three groups of patients received either curcumin (400 milligrams), a placebo (250 mg of lactose powder) or phenylbutazone (100 mg), three times daily for five consecutive days after surgery. They had been admitted for either a hernia condition or an accumulation of fluid in the scrotum. Curcumin was just as effective as phenylbutazone in reducing post-operative inflammation.[4]

Turmeric has also been evaluated as a treatment for inflammation associated with arthritis. Oral administration of curcumin at a dose of 3 mg per kilogram and sodium curcumin at a dose of 0.1 mg/kg inhibited formalin-induced arthritis in rats. In fact, curcumin was comparably effective to phenylbutazone in this application.[5] In another study, oral administration of 0.1 mg/kg of the volatile oil isolated from *Curcuma longa* also decreased arthritis induced in rats.[3]

The antirheumatic properties of curcuminoids were tested in double-blind trial in 49 patients who had been diagnosed with rheumatoid arthritis.[6] When curcumin was given at a dose of 1,200 mg/day for five to six weeks, significant improvement was observed in all patients. There was an overall improvement in morning stiffness and physical endurance. Again, the therapeutic effects were comparable to those obtained with phenylbutazone.

Turmeric was also used to treat patients with chronic respiratory disorders, which resulted in significant relief in symptoms such as cough and shortness of breath.[7] Eye drops prepared from a mixture of turmeric, known as Haridra Eye Drops, were used in 25 cases of an inflammatory condition of the eye, bacterial conjuctivitis.[8] Clinical symptoms such as eye redness or a burning sensation began subsiding after the third day of treatment. During the six-day treatment period, it was determined that 23 of the 25 patients were relieved of all symptoms.

One of the better understood mechanisms of the anti-inflammatory action of curcumin is its inhibition of a group of enzymes which coordinate metabolism of arachidonic acid in the body.[9] Arachidonic acid is an unsaturated fatty acid found in most animal fats, and it is a precursor of prostaglandins. The enzymatic inhibition by curcumin may be a result of diminishing inflammatory products of arachidonic acid metabolism. e.g., postaglandins, leukotrienes and 5-hydroxyeicosatetraenoic acid.[10-12]

Curcumin has a similar action to that of aspirin and aspirin-like anti-inflammatory agents.[13] There is, however, an important advantage for curcumin over aspirin, since curcumin, unlike aspirin, selectively inhibits synthesis of inflammatory prostaglandins but does not affect the synthesis of prostacyclin.[13] Prostacyclin is an important factor in preventing vascular thrombosis, and any drug that affects its synthesis, especially when used in large doses, may increase the risk of this dangerous condition. Curcumin may therefore be preferable for patients who are prone to vascular thrombosis and require anti-inflammatory and/or antiarthritic therapy.

As an antioxidant, curcumin is known to scavenge hydroxyl radicals generated by the inflammatory-response cells (neutrophils), and it also inhibits the production of lipid peroxides, which fuel the inflammatory process.[12,14,15] The anti-inflammatory mechanisms of curcumin are similar to those of phenylbutazone, since there are structural similarities between the two compounds.

In a recent study, researchers using cats evaluated the use of curcumin and quinidine, a standard antiarrhythmic drug, in preventing myocardial ischemia (a condition resulting from the consequences of a heart attack). Both of the substances protected the animals against a decrease in heart rate and blood pressure following restricted blood flow to the heart.[16]

Curcumin may be useful as a new template for the development of better remedies in the prevention of the pathological changes of hardening of the arteries and restenosis (the gradual narrowing of surgically treated arteries.)[17]

CANCER PREVENTION AND TREATMENT

Carcinogens—cancer-causing agents—belong to a diversified group of chemicals which originate from food, food contaminants, food additives, food processing agents, environmental pollutants, synthetic chemicals, pharmaceutical drugs and cosmetics. The development of cancer is a multistep process involving many factors. Cancer-causing agents can either initiate or promote tumors or act as complete carcinogens having both tumor-initiating and -promoting activity. Turmeric and curcuminoids have been found to be cancer-preventing compounds in different tumor models as well as in limited human studies.

As an example, supplementation of one percent turmeric in the daily diet inhibited benzopyrene-induced (benzopyrene is a highly toxic chemical in cigarette smoke which can cause stomach cancer) stomach tumors and in addition, mammary (breast) tumors in mice.[1,2] Also, feeding a water extract of turmeric inhibited stomach tumors in mice.[2-4] In another study, mice fed up to two percent curcumin in their daily diet before and after the onset of stomach cancer showed, in both instances, a reduction in the rate of tumor development.[5] Rats fed with 0.2 percent curcumin in their daily diet showed inhibition of the process leading to the development of colon carcinoma[6,7] (a cancerous, malignant growth in the colon).

In clinical studies, a topical ointment containing five percent curcumin applied to cancerous growth on the skin in 62 patients was found to reduce foul smell, itching, pain and the discharge of fluid from the lesion (wound) in a significant majority of the patients.[8] The foul odor was considerably reduced in more than 90 percent of the patients; pain and itching subsided in 50 percent; and fluid discharge was reduced in 70 percent of the cases.

Turmeric extract alone or in combination with betel leaf extract was effective against tumors induced by a powerful carcinogen (a nitrosamine derivative) in the mouth mucosa of hamsters.[9] Curcumin also inhibited the action of another potent carcinogen (a nitroquinoline derivative) in inducing tumors in the mouth mucosa of rats.[10] In a clinical study, the effectiveness of curcumin was tested in patients with oral cancer. One hundred patients were given 500 mg of curcumin three times a day for 30 days. A significant number of patients improved on the curcumin regimen and responded with dramatic clinical improvement within 15 days, while others responded more gradually throughout the 30-day treatment period.[11]

In a laboratory study in which mice were challenged with carcinogens, curcumin not only inhibited the frequency of tumors, but also reduced tumor sizes in the entire gastrointestinal tract, including the stomach, duodenum and colon.[12] Based on this and similar laboratory studies, curcumin appears to be a promising dietary agent that may improve chances against some forms of cancer.[13] This observation is particularly important since turmeric, a rich source of curcuminoids, is a well-established culinary item in India.

The anticarcinogenic activity of turmeric extract and curcuminoids may be in part explained by their well-researched ability to prevent genetic mutation, or mutagenesis (an alteration in genetic material). Mutation is a genetic change within the "command center" of a cell which is ultimately passed on to subsequent cell generations. This altered regeneration may result in uncontrollable cell growth, as in the case of cancer. As an example of its antimutagenic properties, curcuminoids inhibited capsaicin-induced mutagenic changes in the bone marrow of mice[14] (bone marrow is responsible for the production of new blood cells). Mice maintained on turmeric or curcuminoid enriched diets, when challenged with carcinogens, excreted low levels of mutagenic metabolites as well as carcinogens.[15,16] This and other experimental data show that carcinogens and mutagens could be neutralized by the action of curcuminoids.[17-19]

In a clinical study, curcumin was evaluated as an antimutagen in a group of 16 chronic smokers in India.[20] It was given in a dose of 1.5 grams a day per person for 30 days. This regimen significantly reduced the urinary excretion of tobacco-related mutagens (by approximately 40 percent in 30 days), probably by enhancing the ability of drug metabolizing enzymes to detoxify carcinogens and mutagens found in cigarette smoke. In addition, an aqueous extract of turmeric also inhibited the biological action of mutagens.[5]

Another important area to consider for curcuminoids' properties as antimutagens and anticarcinogens is in the preparation of food. The nutritional quality of food is known to change with cooking. For example, when cooking at high temperatures, amino acids or links of protein undergo a physicochemical change called pyrolysis (literally heat-induced dissolution of their "raw" structure). As a result various food components may be converted into compounds with mutagenic, carcinogenic or diabetogenic (diabetes-producing) properties. Curcuminoids protect food composition by inhibiting the formation of mutagenic pyrolysates.[15] These results validate the healthful practice of using turmeric as a food additive. It has also been found, as mentioned previously, that turmeric extract and curcumin can inhibit the formation of aflatoxin, a common toxin produced by mold growing on poorly preserved foods.[21]

An excess of nitric oxide, contained in the air we breathe, and its derivatives generated in chronic inflammation, have been shown to induce DNA damage. These compounds are also known as cancer and tumor promoters. The *in vitro* experiments show that curcumin inhibits production of nitric oxide derivatives by as much as 50 percent.

From the discussion in this and previous sections, we see that curcumin is a potent tumor inhibitor and chemopreventative agent against cancer, also exhibiting anti-inflammatory and antioxidant activities.[22] Detailed studies have demonstrated that both curcumin and vitamin C (ascorbic acid) possess antioxidant and anticancer properties. Ascorbic acid and curcumin may, therefore, have an additive role in providing protection against cancer.[23,24]

TURMERIC AND AIDS

Human immunodeficiency virus (HIV) infection, which causes acquired immunodeficiency syndrome (AIDS), exemplifies an immune-system disease whose therapy is currently approached in two different ways. One possible approach is through biological response modifiers (BRMs), which work to restore the immune system's ability to defend the body against disease. The other approach is to develop a vaccine against the HIV infection.

Curcuminoids from turmeric are among the most studied natural compounds currently undergoing intensive laboratory and clinical evaluation as anti-HIV biological response modifiers.

The preliminary clinical report presented in 1994 at the International Conference on AIDS in San Francisco discusses the results of curcumin therapy in HIV-infected patients.[1] In this study 18 HIV-positive volunteers took an average of 2000 mg of curcumin per day for an average of 127 days. The study group consisted of 17 men and one woman, and represented 7 patients without clinical symptoms and 11 patients with clinically manifested disease. This study group was matched with the HIV-positive control group. The average age of the treated group was 41.3 years old, while the control group's was 42.8 years. The immune system cell (lymphocyte) count, typically much lower (hence immunodeficiency) in the AIDS patients, was determined before and after the therapy. The lymphocyte count was a criterion for the effectiveness of the treatment.

The CD-4 and CD-8 cells are acronyms for the immune cells called T lymphocytes, which are responsible for some of the most sophisticated activity of the immune system. The

T lymphocytes function like the chief of staff (who presides over a group of generals) to regulate the entire immune response. With regard to this regulatory function, the T lymphocytes can be divided into T helper (CD-4) and T suppressor (CD-8) lymphocytes. T helpers stimulate the immune response, particularly to provide protection against invading microorganisms. The function of T suppressors is to stop this action when appropriate (e.g., when infection has been overcome) to avoid excessive immune system activity being turned against the body itself. Balanced interaction between T helper and T suppressor cells represents self-regulation of the immune response. Self-regulation is regarded as the most crucial aspect of this response.

In HIV infection and especially with the clinically manifested disease of the immune system, AIDS, T helper or CD-4 cells become a primary target of the infection, being increasingly incapacitated and destroyed by the virus. The current definition of AIDS includes HIV infection with CD-4 cell counts lower than 200 per ml of blood. The immune system of the patients who have low counts of CD-4 cells is usually unable to defend the body against various viral, bacterial and parasitic infections. The microorganisms take advantage of the weakened defense system and invade the body; hence those infections are referred to as opportunistic infections.

In the above-cited study, the administration of curcumin to the 18 HIV-infected patients for approximately 20 weeks resulted in a significant increase in the CD-4 (p=0.029) and CD-8 (p=0.009) cell counts, as compared to the placebo-receiving patients. (The CD-4 cell count before the treatment ranged from 5 to 615 cells/ml of blood and the respective range for CD-8 cells count was 283 to 1467 cells/ml of blood.) In conclusion, the authors of this preliminary report found curcumin a safe and effective treatment for HIV infected patients with lowered CD-4 and CD-8 cell counts.

The laboratory studies of turmeric derivatives indicate possible mechanisms by which curcumin compounds may interfere with the HIV infection, preventing the demise of critical CD-4 and CD-8 lymphocytes. HIV is an absolute parasite which cannot live without being fully integrated in the live body cell. The process of acquiring housing in body cells by the virus is that of deadly infection with HIV. The important steps of that process are integration of the virus genetic material (facilitated by the enzyme integrase) with the genetic material of the cell—the command center of vital processes in the cell. Once this integration is completed, the genetic material of the cell is serving the virus, not the cell, which leads to the demise of the "rudderless cell," e.g., death of CD-4 and CD-8 cells. In a 1995 published study, curcumin was found to inhibit the activity of the enzyme integrase, thus potentially preventing HIV from finding a home in CD-4 and/or CD-8 cells.[2]

Another laboratory study indicates that curcumin may work by breaking the self-perpetuating vicious circle in the HIV-infected cell.[3] This mechanism starts when the infected cell is stimulated to produce certain factors called cytokines (nuclear factor-kappa B, tumor necrosis factor and interleukin-1) which promote HIV buildup in the cell. A 1995 study from Rutgers University shows that curcumin in an *in vitro* study at 5 μM concentration may inhibit cytokine production in certain human cells. The author of this communication suggests that the anti-cytokine activity of curcumin may explain a therapeutic potential of this compound not only in HIV infection but in a host of inflammatory conditions which thrive on excess production of cytokines.

The importance of studies of the turmeric derivatives as potential anti-HIV biological response modifiers is obvious. The World Health Organization reported in 1994 that some 17 million people have been infected with HIV worldwide. Approximately 90 percent of those infections occurred in developing countries, with the number of reported AIDS cases up sharply in the US in 1993. In the United States alone AIDS had claimed more than 250,000 lives by the end of 1994.

The vaccine solution to prevent HIV infections is still a remote possibility, particularly in view of the fact that HIV mutates very rapidly. This means that developing resistance through vaccination to one form of HIV may be rendered futile when a new form of HIV evolves. It is noteworthy that some forms of HIV became resistant to the specific antiviral mechanism offered by one of the few useful anti-HIV agents, azidothymidine (AZT).

Turmeric derivatives, on the other hand, may offer in the battle against HIV a nonspecific mechanism or mechanisms that may regulate the immunological response in the direction of natural resistance of the organism to being infected by the virus. Interestingly, the nonspecific or bioprotectant nature of curcuminoids may be studied as an independent therapy modality against the HIV infection, as well as an add-on to specific antiviral drugs, possibly diminishing their inherent toxicity.

PROTECTIVE PROPERTIES OF CURCUMINOIDS

The recently discovered properties—antioxidant, anti-inflammatory, anticancer and antimutagenic—of curcuminoids can best be characterized as protective. This quality of turmeric, exploited in its traditional role as a food preservative, proves that the spice protects the integrity of biomolecules in the body. Interestingly, preventing the deterioration of food and keeping integrated nutrients in tissues from degenerating appear to be closely related. For example, the properties in turmeric which prevent rancidity in meat help to provide edible animal protein that contains less oxidized fat or free radicals. When this type of food is ingested, it supplies "clean" nutrients rather than free radical-damaged nutrients.

Researchers believe that the same attributes of turmeric that preserve the freshness of the food we eat may also protect living tissue from being exposed to degenerative disease. Clinical and laboratory research indicate that diets supplemented with turmeric or curcuminoids stabilize and protect biomolecules in the body.[1,2] This stabilizing effect can be illustrated by the antioxidant, cancer-preventing and mutation-preventing actions of curcuminoids, both under *in vitro* and *in vivo* conditions.[3]

Turmeric and its active principles, the curcuminoids, can exert protection in two ways: directly, by shielding the biomolecular functioning of the body; or indirectly, by increasing its waste removal action, and also by boosting immune system function. As an example, feeding curcuminoids to laboratory animals resulted in elevated levels of the enzyme glutathione S-transferase, an important index of the efficiency of detoxification.[2,4,-7] Such systematic cleansing processes help to preserve the integrity of biological systems.

In addition to preserving the nutritional value of food and protecting the body from damaging free radicals, curcuminoids ameliorate side effects of treatment with chemotherapeutic agents.[8] Turmeric extract and curcuminoids were tested for their ability to prevent tissue damage by some anticancer drugs and environmental toxins and pollutants. Anticancer drugs were generally more effective and less toxic when used in combination with turmeric or curcuminoids. Similarly, laboratory animals subjected to an environmental toxin such as aflatoxin benefited from diets that were enriched with turmeric extract or curcuminoids.[9] Toxic effects produced by aflatoxin were significantly diminished by the curcuminoid supplementation.

Curcuminoids also play a significant role *in vitro* in protecting some drugs from breakdown of their physical and chemical aspects. For instance, adding curcumin to nifedipine (a cardiovascular drug) prevented degradation of the drug due to ultraviolet light.[10] This protective effect increased as larger concentrations of curcumin were added to the nifedipine preparations. This drug is a calcium channel blocker used to treat angina pectoris, a form of cardiovascular disease.

It is therefore evident that curcuminoids deserve special attention as compounds that protect biological systems internally and externally from the deterioration associated with aging, disease and drug-related side effects.

SAFETY OF CURCUMINOIDS

For centuries, turmeric has been used as a food additive, a medicinal agent, and a dye for cosmetics and fabrics without manifesting side effects. This record of safety has been one of the deciding factors that allowed the Food and Agricultural Organization/World Health Organization (FAO/WHO) expert committee on food additives to approve curcuminoids as natural food coloring agents.[1,2] Turmeric is listed by the U.S. Food and Drug Administration as an herb Generally Recognized as Safe (GRAS)—21 CFR 100.00. 182.10 and 182.20—for its intended use as a spice, seasoning and flavoring agent.

The safety of *Curcuma longa* and its derivatives have been studied in various animal models. A single feeding of a 30 percent turmeric diet to rats did not produce any toxic effects.[3] In a 24-hour acute toxicity study, mice were fed dosages of 0.5 gram, 1 gram and 3 g/kg of turmeric extract and in a 90-day chronic toxicity study, mice were fed drinking water containing 100 mg/kg turmeric extract daily.[4] There was no increase in mortality rate when compared to the respective controls in either study. The 90-day treatment with turmeric extract resulted in no significant overall weight gain. Interestingly, as a result of the 90-day treatment with turmeric extract, there was an increase in the weight of sexual organs and enhancement in sperm motility. Writing in the *Indian Journal of Experimental Biology*, the researchers concluded that turmeric is not toxic even at the high doses that they gave to laboratory animals.[5]

ORIGIN AND VARIETIES OF TURMERIC

A native of South and Southeast Asia, turmeric probably originated on the slopes of hills in the tropical forests of the Western Ghats of South India. *Curcuma* consists of more than 100 species and several varieties of rhizomatous herbs grown extensively in East and Southeast Asia. The commonly used ginger, *Zingiber officinale Rosc.*, is also an economically important member of the same family.

Curcuma can be grown in a diverse tropical environment, ranging from sea level to a height of 5,000 feet, on hilly slopes and in temperatures ranging from 68 to 86° Fahrenheit (20 to 30° Celsius). A rainfall of 60 inches per annum or more in the growing regions, or an equivalent amount of irrigation, is essential. Loose, loamy or alluvial soil suitable for irrigation and efficient drainage is necessary.

Along with ginger, turmeric was probably taken from India to Southeast Asia (Indonesia, Thailand, Malay archipelago), China and northern Australia, and then to the West Indies and South America by Spanish explorers. Subsequently its cultivation spread to many African countries. There is no available documented literature about the methods of cultivation in areas other than India. Since India remains the largest producer of turmeric, its acreage and production exceeds the total of all other growing countries, except for China and Indonesia, for which current figures are not available.[1]

Curcuma longa is looked upon as one of the most important species because of its commercial value and extensive research data which shows diverse therapeutic significance.

Like other members of the Zingiberaceae family, *Curcuma longa L.* is a typical herbaceous plant with thick and fleshy rhizomes and leaves in sheaths. The plants reach a height of up to three feet. Dark green leaves, either obliquely erect or oblong, are shaped like a lance head, tapering near the leaf and broadening near the base and enveloping the succeeding shoot. Flowers can sometimes be seen on cylindrical spikes bearing numerous greenish-white bracts. The flowers are narrow and yellowish-white in color.

The underground rhizome, which is processed into the commercial varieties, consists of two distinct parts:[2]

1. The egg-shaped primary or mother rhizome, which is an extension of the stem and forms the bulbs—C. *rotunda* of Western commerce.

2. Several egg-shaped, oblong or pyriform or cylindrical multibranched rhizomes growing downward from the primary rhizome, which form the C. *longa* of commerce.

Several varieties of *Curcuma longa* under cultivation have evolved through natural selection. Besides some varieties which have been known since ancient times, more than 30 new varieties are grown in India. Several new varieties have also adapted to cultivation in South America and the West Indies in recent years.

The curcuminoid content of turmeric is responsible for color intensity and depends upon the variety and maturity of the rhizome at the time of harvest.[3,4] For example, the variation in curcumin content for three kinds of C. *longa* at maturity is as follows:

Harvest	Percent Total Color as Curcumin		
	WYNAD	KARHADI	KUCHIPUDI
September	3.8	4.3	4.1
October	5.0	4.8	4.2
November	n.a.	4.9	3.8
December	5.8	4.0	3.0
January	3.8	3.5	2.1

The important considerations for the grower to obtain a good commercial quality of turmeric include the selection of varieties according to the following criteria: color, aroma, yield and resistance to diseases and pests

Varieties such as Tekkurpetta and Rajpore yield 30-33 tons of green turmeric per kilohectare (about 2500 acres). The curcumin content of commonly grown Indian varieties varies from 2.5 percent to 8.1 percent on a dry-matter basis, while volatile oil content, which provides aroma, varies from 1.8 to 5.6 percent on a dry-matter basis.[3] Yields are reported to improve considerably with the use of nitrogen, phosphorus and potassium fertilizer.

Harvesting of the rhizomes at the right maturity is important for optimum color and aroma. Before harvest, the leaves and stems are cut close to the ground and the field left dry to facilitate digging out the rhizomes with a plow or hoe. The rhizome branches are carefully lifted, adhering soil is removed by soaking in water, and a further cleansing of roots and scales is done before they are dispatched to the curing yard.

Green turmeric is cured and dried for commercial use. Processing includes boiling for periods ranging from 30 minutes to three hours (which reduces the drying time without affecting color or volatile oil content) or peeling and slicing (which results in low moisture content, useful in the manufacture of turmeric powder), followed by drying. The semi-dried product is prone to microbiological damage, hence washing, curing and drying help to reduce the microbial load. Boiling helps to increase the rate of drying and provides a hard, filled (not wrinkled) product which can be polished easily. Slicing reduces processing costs and is used for material intended for oleoresin or powder manufacture. The commercial product is in the form of dried bulbs, fingers or powders.

Cured and dried turmeric for commercial use, both bulb and finger forms, is bright yellow or dull yellow in color, with a polished or rough surface. The bulb form is usually 3 centimeters in diameter and 4 to 5 centimeters long, while the fingers are tapering cylinders 2.5 to 7.5 centimeters in length and 7 to 15 millimeters thick. Both have a number of transverse rings, root scars and cut surfaces at areas where there are two growth forms and the secondary branches are separated. When cut or fractured, the break is clean and not splintering or fibrous. The cut surface of the fresh rhizome is waxy and resinous in appearance.

In the transverse cut surface, the endoderm is clearly seen as a light yellow circle separating the dark yellow cortex and central cylinder. Due to the boiling during the curing process, there is usually some spread of an orange-yellow or brownish-yellow color over the entire surface.

CHEMICAL CONSTITUENTS OF TURMERIC

A yellow-pigmented fraction isolated from the rhizomes of *Curcuma longa* contains curcuminoids belonging to the dicinnamoyl methane group. Curcuminoids are present to the extent of three to five percent. Curcumin (or more specifically, a mixture of curcuminoids) is an important active ingredient responsible for the biological activity of *Curcuma longa*. Although its main activity is anti-inflammatory, it has also been reported to possess antioxidant, antiallergic, wound healing, antispasmodic, antibacterial and antitumor activity.[1,2] A recent research project at Harvard Medical School indicated that curcuminoids (in the form of C^3 Complex) may processes anti-HIV activity as well.[3]

Curcumin was isolated as early as 1815. It is insoluble in water but soluble in ethanol and acetone. Daube in 1870 obtained it in crystalline form.[4] The structure of curcumin as a diferuloylmethane was confirmed with the initial work and synthesis by Lampe in 1910.[5,6]

Based on the following findings, the structure of curcumin was established as diferuloylemethane:

1. Using boiling water and an alkali, curcumin released vanillic acid and ferulic acid.

2. Fusing with an alkali produced protocatechuic acid.

3. Oxidation with the potassium salt permanganate, yielded vanillin, which is usually extracted from vanilla beans and used in flavoring and in perfumery.

4. A characteristic isoxazole derivative was obtained when curcumin was treated with hydroxylamine.

5. Curcumin also formed a diacetyl derivative, and on

hydrogenation, a mixture of hexahydro and tetrahydro derivatives.

Srinivasan, while attempting to estimate curcumin in turmeric, observed that the color obtained with turmeric extract was slightly different from that obtained with pure curcumin.[7] The solution exhibited an orange fluorescence with turmeric extract, which was absent in the reference solution. He came to the conclusion that there must be one or more substances in turmeric besides curcumin which were responsible for this fluorescence.

Srinivasan carried out chromatographic analysis of pigments in turmeric and isolated two new components. The molecular weight, methoxyl values, chemical reactions, absorption spectrum, etc., showed that these two compounds are related to curcumin, and they have been named demethoxycurcumin and bisdemethoxycurcumin. Recently a new curcuminoid, cyclocurcumin, was isolated from turmeric.[8]

CONCLUDING THOUGHTS

Antioxidants of different kinds have always been with us in one form or another. For thousands of years people have consumed them in the foods that contain them without ever realizing the nutritional good they were doing themselves. Until quite recently free radicals were an unknown quantity in the health equation. But a mountain of research has shown that these misguided molecules are responsible for much of the accelerated aging we see in our society today. Free radicals also play an inconspicuous but important part in many of the health problems accompanying old age.

Turmeric is an ancient spice that dates back to the time of the Egyptian pharaohs and Indian rajas. It has been utilized for a very long time as a food flavoring and medicinal agent. But now scientific research has unlocked some of its wonderful "anti-aging," wellness-promoting secrets. They come in the form of antioxidant compounds collectively known as curcuminoids. Independently, they work hard to curb free radical activity. But taken in group arrangements such as C^3 Complex, they are three times as potent in checking the negative behavior of these errant molecules. When taken into the system on a regular basis, *unified* curcuminoids can accomplish miraculous things that will leave the human body feeling dynamic and looking terrific.

NOTES

Introduction

1. Dymock, W., et al. (1972). *Pharmacographica Indica*, Hamdard 1 Reddy, A.C.P., and Lokesh, B.R. (1992). "Studies on Spice Principles as Antioxidants in the Inhibition of Lipid Peroxidation of Rat Liver Microsomes," *Mol. Cell. Biochem.* 111:117.
2. Lin, J.K., et al. (1994). "Molecular Mechanisms of Action of Curcumin," in *Food Phytochemicals II: Teas, Spices and Herbs*, American Chemical Society 20:196.
3. Kakaiu, H.F., and Iwao, H. (1974). *Jap. J. Nutr.* 32:1
4. Revankar, G.D., and Sen, D.P. (1975). *J. Oil. Tech. Assoc.* 7:88.
5. Arora, R.B., et al. (1971). "Anti-Inflammatory Studies on Curcuma Longa, L.," *Ind. J. Med. Res.* 59:1289.
6. Srimal, R.C., et al. (1971). "A Preliminary Report on Anti-Inflammatory Activity of Curcumin," *Ind. J. Pharmacol.* 3:10.
7. Ghatak, N., and Basu, N. (1972). "Sodium Curcuminate as an Effective Anti-Inflammatory Agent," *Ind. J. Exp. Biol.* 10:235.
8. Li, C.J., et al. (1993). "Three Inhibitors of Human Type I Immundeficiency Virus Long Terminal Repeat Directed Gene Expression and Virus Replication," *Proc. Natl. Acad. Sci., USA*, 90:1839.
9. Copeland, R., et al. (1994). "Curcumin Therapy in HIV-Infected Patients Initially Increased CD-4 and CD-8 Counts," *Int. Conf. AIDS*, Abst. No. PBO876.

Antioxidant Properties

1. Reddy, A.C.P., and Lokesh, B.R. (1992). "Studies on Spice Principles as Antioxidants in the Inhibition of Lipid Peroxidation of Rat Liver Microsomes," *Mol. Cell. Biochem.* 111:117.
2. Sharma, O.P. (1976). "Antioxidant Activity of Curcumin and Related Compounds," *Biochem. Pharmacol.* 25:1811.
3. Sreejayan, and Rao, M.N.A. (1994). "Curcuminoids as Potent Inhibitors of Lipid Peroxidation," *J. Pharm. Pharmacol.* 46:1013.
4. Sharma, S.C. et al. (1972). "Lipid Peroxide Formation in Experimental Inflammation," *Biochem. Pharmacol.* 21:1210.
5. Shih, C.A., and Lin, J.K. (1993). "Inhibition of 8-hydroxydeoxyguanosine Formation by Curcumin in Mouse Fibroblast Cells," *Carcinogenesis* 14:709.
6. Kakaiu, H.F., and Iwao, H. (1974). *Jap. J. Nutr.* 32:1
7. Revankar, G.D., and Sen, D.P. (1975). *J. Oil Tech. Assoc.* 7:88.
8. Anto, R.J., et al. (1994). "A Comparative Study of the Pharmacological Properties of Natural Curcuminoids," *Amala Research Bull.* 14:60.

9. *Research Report No. 786*, Sabinsa Corporation (USA)(1995).

10. Japanese Patent: Kobe Steel KK12.08.88-JP-199949.

11. Srinivas, L., Shalini, V.K., and Shylaja, M. (1992). "Turmerin: A Water-soluble Antioxidant Peptide from Turmeric," *Arch. Biochem. Biophy.* 292:617.

Overview of Laboratory and Clinical Studies

1. Majeed, M., and Badmaev, V. Research Report No. 786. (1995). Sabinsa Corporation, USA. "Antioxidant and Free Radical Trapping Properties of Curcuminoids." Nutracon '95, Las Vegas 1995, July 11-13.

2. Soni, K.B., and Kuttan, R. (1992). "Effect of Oral Curcumin Administration on Serum Peroxides and Cholesterol Levels in Human Volunteers." *Ind. J. Physiol. Pharmacol.* 36:273,293.

3. Ghatak, N., and Basu, N. (1972). "Sodium Curcuminate as an Effective Anti-Inflammatory Agent," *Ind. J. Exp. Biol.* 10:235.

4. Srimal, R.C., and Dhawan, N. (1973). "Pharmacology of Diferuloyl Methane (Curcumin), a Non-Steroidal Anti-Inflammatory Agent," *J. Pharm. Pharmacol.* 25:447.

5. Srimal, R.C., and Dhawan, B.N. (1985). "Pharmacological and Clincial Studies on Curcuma Longa," *Hamdard Nat'l. Found. Monograph*, New Delhi, India, Section 3B(ii) p. 131.

6. Deodhar, S.D., et al. (1980). "Preliminary Studies on Anti-Rheumatic Activity of Curcumin," *Ind. J. Med. Res.* 71:632.

7. Ammon, H.P.T., et al. (1993) "Mechanism of Anti-inflammatory Actions of Curcumin and Boswellic Acids." *J. Ethnopharmacol.* 38:113.

8. Huang, M.T., et al. (1991). "Inhibitory Effects of Curcumin on In Vitro Lipoxygenase and Cyclooxygenase Activities in Mouse Epidermis," *Canc. Res.* 51:813.

9. Rao, C.V., et al. (1993). "Inhibition by Dietary Curcumin of Azoymethane-Induced Ornithine Decarboxylase, Tyrosine Protein Kinase, Arachidonic Acid Metabolism and Aberrant Crypt Foci Formation in the Rat Colon," *Carcinogenesis* 14:2219.

10. Rao, C.V., et al. (1993). "Antioxidant Activity of Curcumin and Related Compounds. Lipid peroxide Formation in Experimental Inflammation," *Cancer Res.* 55:259.

11. Sharma, S.C., et al. (1972). "Lipid Peroxide Formation in Experimental Inflammation," *Biochem. Pharmacol.* 21:1210.

12. Sharma, O.P. (1976). "Antioxidant Activity of Curcumin and Related Compounds," *Biochem. Pharmacol.* 25:1811.

13. Nagabhushan, M., and Bhide, S.V. (1987). "Antimutagenicity and Anticarcinogenicity of Turmeric," *J.Nutr. Growth Canc.* 4:83.

14. Nagabhushan, M. (1987). Ph.D. Thesis, University of Bombay, India.

15. Usha, K., et al. (1994). "The Possible Mode of Actions of Cancer Chemopreventive Spice, Turmeric," *J. Am. Coll. Nutr.* 13:519.

16. Polasa, K., et al. (1992). "Effect of Turmeric on Urinary Mutagens in Urinary Mutagens in Smokers," *Mutagenesis* 7:107.

17. "Turmeric's Anti-Cancer Use." (1992). Press Release, UNI, Hyderabad, India.

18. Ammon, H.P.T., and Wahl, M.A. (1991). "Pharmacology of Curcuma Longa," *Planta Med.* 57:1.

19. Soni, K.B., et al. (1992). "Reversal of Aflatoxin Induced Liver Damage by Turmeric and Curcumin," *Cancer Lett.* 66:115.

20. Rafatullah, S., et al. (1990). "Evaluation of Turmeric (Curcuma Longa) for Gastric and Duodenal Antiulcer Activity in Rats," *J. Ethnopharmacology* 29:25-34.
21. Li, C.J., et al. (1993). "Three Inhibitors of Human Type I Immunodeficiency Virus Long Terminal Repeat Directed Gene Expression and Virus Replication," *Proc. Nat'l. Acad. Sci.* (USA) 90:1839.
22. Copeland, R., et al. (1994). "Curcumin Therapy in HIV-Infected Patients Initially Increased CD-4 and CD-8 Counts," *Int. Conf. AIDS,* Abst. No. PBO876.

Anti-Inflammatory Activity

1. Arora, R.B., et al. (1971). "Anti-inflammatory Studies on Curcuma Longa L.," *Ind. J. Med.* Res. 59:1289.
2. Ghatak, N., and Basu, N. (1972). "Sodium Curcuminate as an Effective Anti-inflammatory Agent," *Ind. J. Exp. Biol.* 10:235.
3. Chandra, D., and Gupta, S.S. (1972). "Anti-Inflammatory and Anti-arthritic Activity of Volatile Oil of C. Longa," *Ind. J. Med. Res.* 60:138.
4. Satoskar, R.R., et al. (1986). "Evaluation of Anti-Inflammatory Property of Curcumin in Patients with Post-Operative Inflammation," *Ind. J. Clin. Pharmacol. Toxicol.* 24:651.
5. Srimal, R.C., and Dhawan, B.N. (1985). "Pharmacological and Clinical Studies on Curcuma Longa," *Hamdard Nat'l. Found. Monograph,* New Delhi, India, Section 3B(ii), p. 131.
6. Deodhar, S.D., et al. (1980). "Preliminary Studies on Anti-Rheumatic Activity of Curcumin," *Ind. J. Med. Res.* 71:632.
7. Jain, J.P., et al. (1979). "Clinical Trials of Haridra in Cases of Tamak Swasa and Kasa," *J. Res. Indian. Med. Yoga and Homeo.* 14:110.
8. Srinvas, C., and Prabhakaran, K.V.S. (1989). *Science of Life* 8:279.
9. Ammon, H.P.T., et al. (1993). "Mechanism of Anti-Inflammatory Actions of Curcumin and Boswellic Acids," *J. Ethnopharmacology* 38:113.
10. Huang, M.T., et al. (1991). "Inhibitory Effects of Curcumin on In Vitro Lipoxygenase and Cyclooxygenase Activities in Mouse Epidermis," *Canc. Res.* 51:813.
11. Rao, C.V., et al. (1993). "Inhibition by Dietary Curcumin of Azoxymethane-Induced Ornithine Decarboxylase, Tyrosine Protein Kinase, Arachidonic Acid Metabolism and Aberrant Crypt Foci Formation in the Rat Colon," *Carcinogenesis* 14:2219.
12. Rao, C.V., et al. (1993). "Antioxidant Activity of Curcumin and Related Compounds. Lipid Peroxide Formation in Experimental Inflammation," *Cancer Res.* 55:259.
13. Srivastava, V., et al. (1986). "Effect of Curcumin on Platelet Aggregation and Vascular Prostacyclin Synthesis," *Arzneim. Forsch./Drug Res.* 36:715.
14. Sharma, S.C., et al. (1972). "Lipid Peroxide Formation in Experimental Inflammation," *Biochem. Pharmacol.* 25:1811.
15. Sharma, O.P. (1976). "Antioxidant Activity of Curcumin and Related Compounds," *Biochem. Pharmacol.* 25:1811.
16. Dikshit, M., et al. (1995). "Prevention of Ischaemia-Induced Biochemical Changes in Curcumin and Quinidine in the Cat Heart," *Ind. J. Med. Res.* 101:31-35.
17. Huang, Huei-Chen, et al. (1992). "Inhibitory Effect of Curcumin, an Anti-Inflammatory Agent on Vascular Smooth Muscle Cell Proliferation," *Eur. J. Pharmacol.* 221:381-384.

Cancer Prevention and Treatment

1. Nagabhushan, M., and Bhide, S.V. (1987). "Antimutagenicity and Anticarcinogenicity of Turmeric," *J. Nutr. Growth Canc.* 4:83.

2. Nagabhushan, M., (1987). PhD. Thesis, Universtiy of Bombay, India.

3. Nagabhushan, M., and Bhide, S.V. (1992). "Curcumin as an Inhibitor of Cancer," *J. Am. Coll. Nutr.* 11:192.

4. Huang, M.T., et al. (1991). "Inhibitory Effects of Curcumin on In Vitro Lipoxygenase and Cyclooxygenase Activities in Mouse Epidermis," *Cancer Res.* 51:813.

5. Azuine, M.A., et al. (1992). "Protective Role of Aqueous Turmeric Extract Against Mutagenicity of Direct-Acting Carcinogens as Well as Benzo (Alpha) Pyrene-Induced Genotoxicity and Carcinogenicity," *J. Canc. Res. Clin. Oncol.* 118:447.

6. Rao, C.V., et al. (1993). "Inhibition by Dietary Curcumin of Azoxymethane-Induced Ornithine Decarboxylase, Tyrosine Protein Kinase, Arachidonic Acid Metabolism and Aberrant Crypt Foci Formation in the Rat Colon," *Carcinogenesis* 14:2219.

7. Rao, C.V., et al. (1995). "Chemoprevention of Colon Carcinogenesis by Dietary Curcumin, a Naturally Occurring Plant Phenolic Compound," *Cancer Res.* 55:259.

8. Kuttan, R., et al. (1987). "Turmeric and Curcumin as Topical Agents in Cancer Therapy," *Tumori* 2/28:29.

9. Azuine, M.A., and Bhide, S.V. (1992). "Protective Single/Combined Treatment with Betel Leaf and Turmeric Against Methyl (Acetoxymethyl) Nitrosamine-Induced Hamster Oral Carcinogenesis," *Int. J. Canc.* 51:412-415.

10. Tanaka, T., et al. (1994). "Chemoprevention of 4-Nitroquinoline-1-Oxide-Induced Oral Carcinogenesis By Dietary Curcumin and Hesperidin: Comparison with the Protective Effect of Beta-Carotene," *Canc. Res.* 54:4653.

11. *Turmeric's Anti-Cancer Use* (1992). Press Release (UNI) Hyderabad, India.

12. Huang, M.T., et al. "Inhibitory Effect of Curcumin on Tumorigenesis in Mice," International Symposium on Curcumin Pharmacochemistry, Aug. 29-31, 1995, Gadjahmada University, Yogyakarta, Indonesia.

13. Brouet, I., and Ohshima, H. (1995). "Curcumin, An Anti-Tumour Promoter and Anti-Inflammatory Agent, Inhibits Induction of Nitric Oxide Synthase in Activated Macrophages," *Biochem. and Biophys. Res. Comm.* 20(6):533-540.

14. Sarkar, S., et al. (1988). *Anticancer Research* 16:1055.

15. Usha, K., et al. (1994). "The Possible Mode of Action of Cancer Chemopreventive Spice, Turmeric," *J. Am. Coll. Nutr.* 13:519.

16. Polasa, K., et al. (1991). "Curcuma Longa-Induced Reduction in Urinary Mutagens," *Food Chem. Toxicol.* 29:699.

17. *Annual Report* (1984). Cancer Res. Inst., Bombay, India.

18. Nagabhushan, M., et al. (1987). "In Vitro Antimutagenicity of Curcumin Against Environmental Mutagens," *Food Chem. Toxicol.* 25:545.

19. Nagabhushan, M., et al. (1987). *Ind. Drugs* 25:1

20. Polasa, K., et al. (1992). "Effect of Turmeric on Urinary Mutagens in Smokers," *Mutagenesis* 7:107.

21. Madhyastha, M.S., and Bhat, R.V. (1985). "Evaluation of Substrate Potentiality and Inhibitory Effects to Identify High Risk Spices for Aflatoxin Contamination," *J. Food Sci.* 50:376.

22. Ruby, A.J., et al. (1995). "Anti-Tumor and Antioxidant Activity of Natural Curcuminoids," *Cancer Letters* 94:79-83.

23. Huang, M.T., et al. (1992). "Effect of Dietary Curcumin and Ascorbyl Palmitate

on Azoxymethanol-Induced Colonic Epithelial Cell Proliferation and Focal Areas of Dysplasia," *Cancer Letters* 64:117-121.

24. Sahu, Saura C., and Washington, Melissa C. (1992). "Effect of Ascorbic Acid and Curcumin on Quercetin-Induced Nuclear DNA Damage, Lipid Peroxidation and Protein Degradation," *Cancer Letters* 63:237-241.

Turmeric and AIDS

1. Copeland, R., Baker, D., Wilson, II, (1994), "Curcumin Therapy in HIV-Infected Patients Initially Increased CD-4 and CD-8 Cell Counts," In. *Conf. AIDS*, 10(2):216 (abstract no. PB0876).

2. Mazumder, A., et al. (1995). "Inhibition of Human Immunodeficiency Virus Type-1 Integrase by Curcumin." *Biochem. Pharmacol.*, 49(8):1165-1170.

3. Chan, MM-Y, (1995) "Inhibition of Tumor Necrosis by Curcumin, a Phytochemical," *Biochem. Pharmacol.*, 49(11):1551-1556.

Protective Properties of Curcuminoids

1. Mukundan, M.A., et al. (1992). "Effect of Turmeric and Curcumin on BP-DNA Adducts," *Carcinogenesis* 14:493.

2. Lahiri, M., and Bhide, S.V. (1993). "Effect of Four Plant Phenols, Beta-Carotene and Alpha-Tocopherol on 3(H)benzopyrene-DNA Interaction in vitro in the Presence of Rat and Mouse Liver Postmitochondrial Fraction," *Cancer Lett.* 73:35.

3. Ammon, H.P.T., and Wahl, M.A. (1991). "Pharmacology of Curcuma Longa," *Planta Med.* 57:1.

4. Susan, M., and Rao, M.N.A. (1992). "Induction of Glutathione S-Transferase Activity by Curcumin in Mice," *Arzheim Foresh.* 42:962.

5. Goud, V.K., et al. (1993). "Effect of Turmeric on Xenobiotic Metabolizing Enzymes," *Plant Food Hum. Nutr.* 44:87.

6. Goud, V.K., and Krishnaswamy, K. (1993). "Mechanism of Anticarcinogenesis of Curcumin and Turmeric," *Symposium on Therapeutic Potential of Turmeric and Curcumin, NIH,* Hyderabad, India.

7. Aruna, K., and Sivaramakrishan, V.M. (1992). "Anticarcinogenic Effects of Some Indian Plant Products," *J.Food Chem. Toxicol.* 30:953.

8. Soudamani, K.K., and Kuttan, R. (1992). "Chemoprotective Effects of Curcumin Against Cyclophosphamide Toxicity," *Ind. J. Pharm. Sci.* 54:213. and Soudamini, K.K., and Kuttan, R. (1989). "Inhibition of Chemical Carcinogenesis by Curcumin," *J. Ethnopharmacol.* 27:227.

9. Soni, K.B., et al. (1992). "Reversal of Aflatoxin-Induced Liver Damage by Turmeric and Curcumin," *Cancer Lett.* 66:115.

10. Ali, A., and Sharma, S.N. (1992). "Stabilization of Nifedipine Preparations with Curcumin," *Ind. J. Pharm. Sci.* 54:101.

Safety of Curcuminoids

1. WHO (1976). *Food Additives* 7:75.

2. WHO (1961). *Food Additives* 70:40.

3. *Report on Toxicity of Curcumin, CDRI,* Lucknow, India (1977).

4. Qureshi, S., et al. (1992). "Toxicity Studies on Alpinia Galanga and Curcuma Longa," *Planta Medica* 58:124.

5. Bhavani Shankar, T.N. et al. (1980). "Toxicity Studies on Turmeric: Acute Toxicity Studies in Rats, Guinea Pigs and Monkeys," *Indian J. Exp. Biol.* 18:73.

Origin and Varieties of Turmeric

1. Paulose, T.T., and Velappan, E. (1974). "Future Prospects for Spice Industry," *Proc. Symp. Development Prospects of Spice Industry in India*, Assoc. Food Sci. Tech. (India), P.78.
2. Melchior, H., and Kastner, H. (1974). "Curcuma," in *Gewurz, Botaniche und Chemische Untersuchng*, Verlag, Paul Paray, Berlin, P. 157.
3. Govindarajan, V.S. (1980). "Turmeric—Chemistry, Technology and Quality," in *CRC Critical Reviews in Food Science and Nutrition* 12:200.
4. Cooray, N.F., et al. (1988). "Effect of Maturity on Some Chemical Constituents of Turmeric," *J. Natl. Sci. Coun.*, Sri Lanka 16:39.

Chemical Constituents of Turmeric

1. Srimal, R.C. (1987). "Curcumin in Drugs of the Future" 12:331.
2. Polasa, K., Sesikaran, B., and Krishnaswamy, K. (1990). "Antimutagenicity of Curcumin and Turmeric," *Proceedings of the Nutritional Society of India* 36:102.
3. *AIDS Treatment News.* (1993), 176:1.
4. Vogel and Pelletier. (1818). *J. Pharm.* 2:50. Also, Daube, F.V. (1870). *Uber Curcumin, den Farbstoff der Curcumawurzel, Ber.* 3:609.
5. Lampe, V., et al. (1910). *Ber. Dtsch Chem. Ges.* 43:2163.
6. Lampe, V., and Milobedzka, J. (1913). *Ber. Dtsch, Chem. Ges.* 46:2235. Cited by Rougley and Whiting (1971), in "Diarylheptanoids: the Problems of Biosynthesis," *Tetrahedron Letters* 40:5741.
7. Srinivasan, K.R. (1952). "The Coloring Matter in Turmeric," *Current Science*, p. 311.
8. Kiuchi, F., et al. (1993). "Nematocidal Activity of Turmeric: Synergistic Action of Curcuminoids," *Chem. Pharm. Bull.* 41:1640.